Finding Africa

by Jamie A. Schroeder

Table of Contents

Where Is Africa?.....................4
What Is a Map Key?................6
What Symbols Are on Maps?..........8
How Can You Find Symbols
 with a Map Key?..................10
Glossary and Index 16

I need to know these words.

Africa

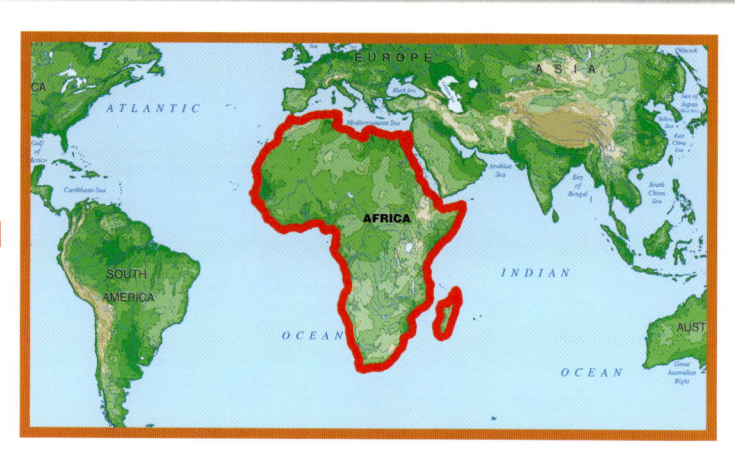

continents

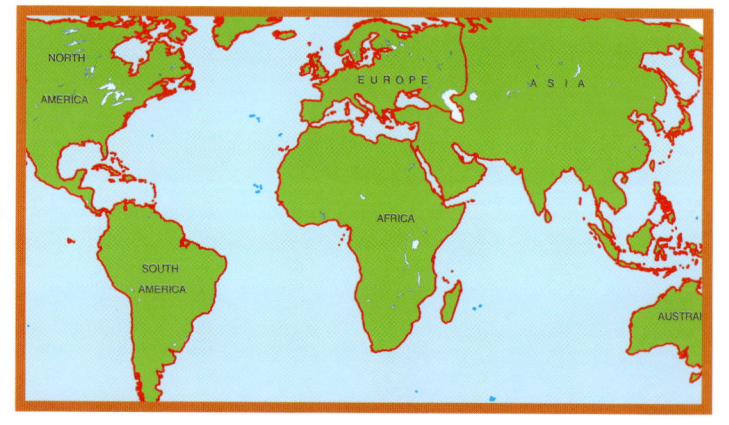

desert

map key

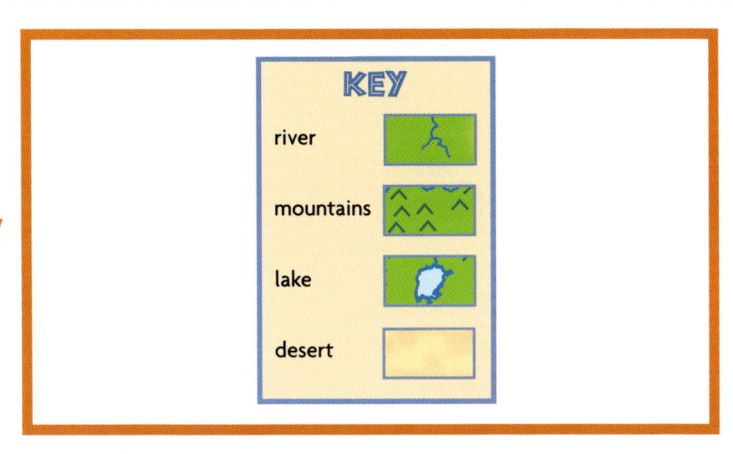

KEY
river
mountains
lake
desert

river

symbols

3

Where Is Africa?

Look at the map. Can you find Africa on the map? Africa is a large **continent**.

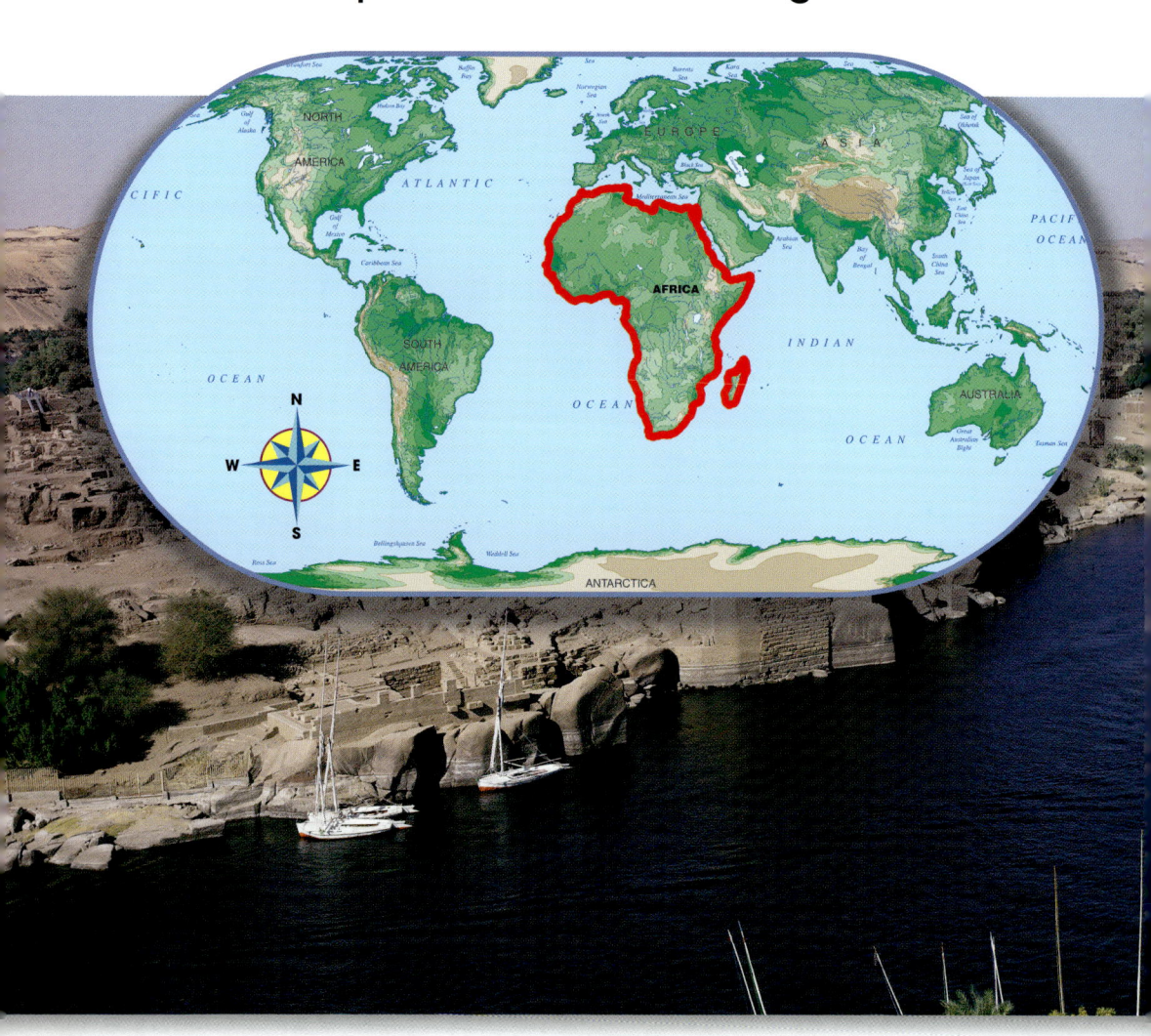

A map can help you find Africa.
A map can help you find places
in Africa. A map can help you find
the Nile River in Africa.

▲ The Nile River is about 4,000 miles long.

What Is a Map Key?

Most maps have a **map key**. A map key has **symbols** and words. The words tell you what the symbols mean. Use the map key to find the Nile River.

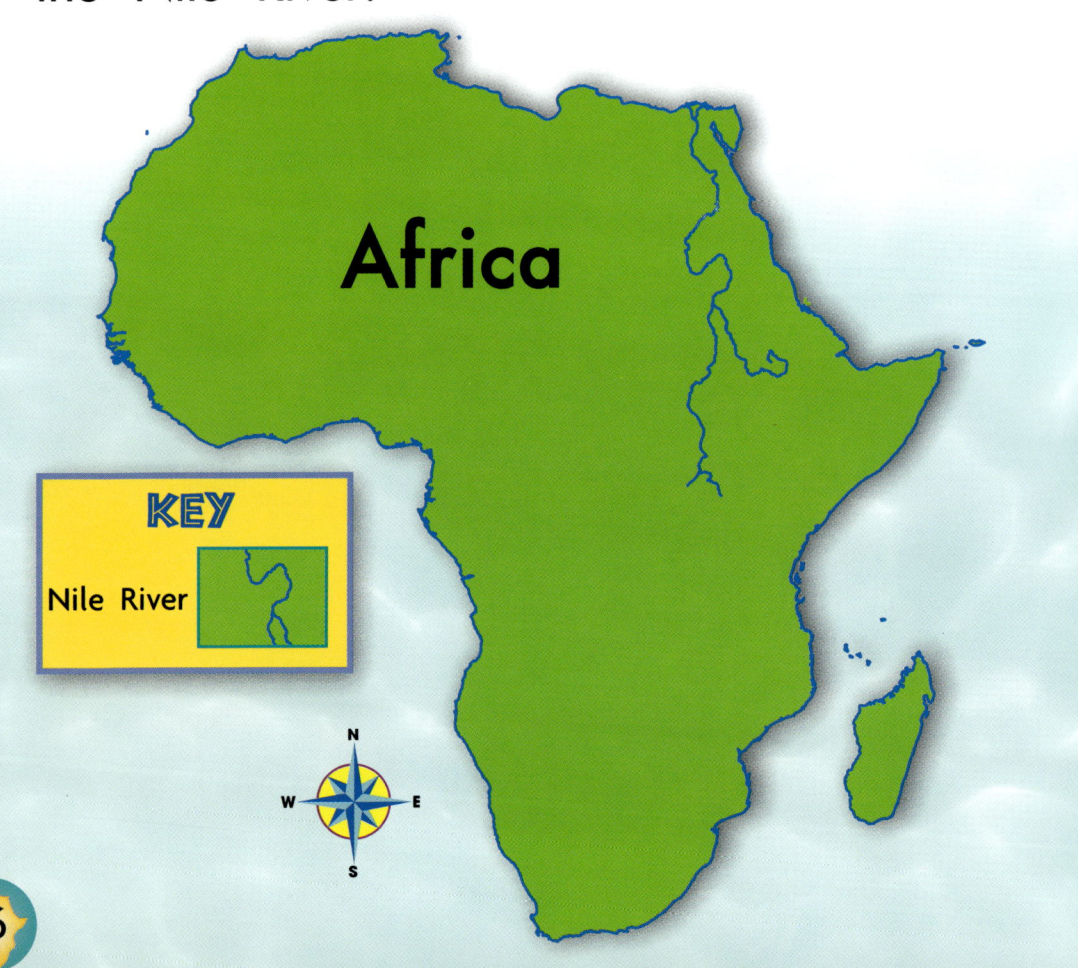

What Is a Symbol?

A mapmaker draws small pictures on maps. These pictures are symbols. A symbol is a drawing that means a word.

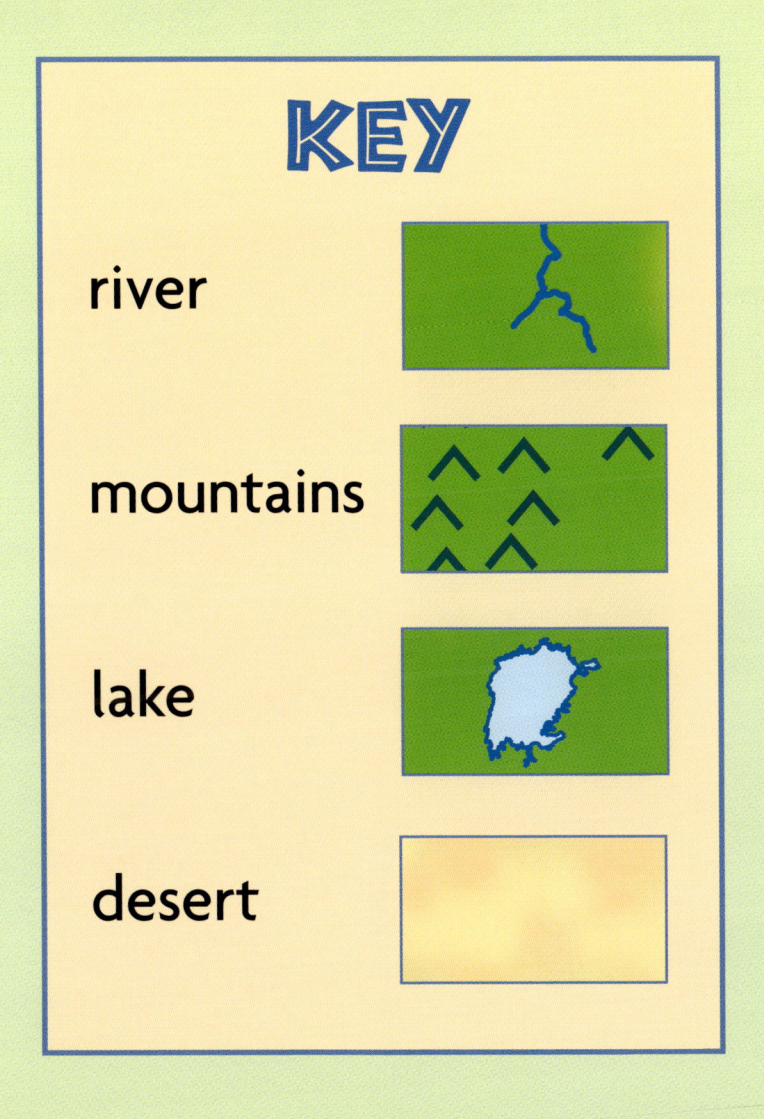

KEY

river	
mountains	
lake	
desert	

What Symbols Are on Maps?

A map key can show symbols of **landforms**. A map can show symbols of mountains. A map can show symbols of lakes and rivers, too.

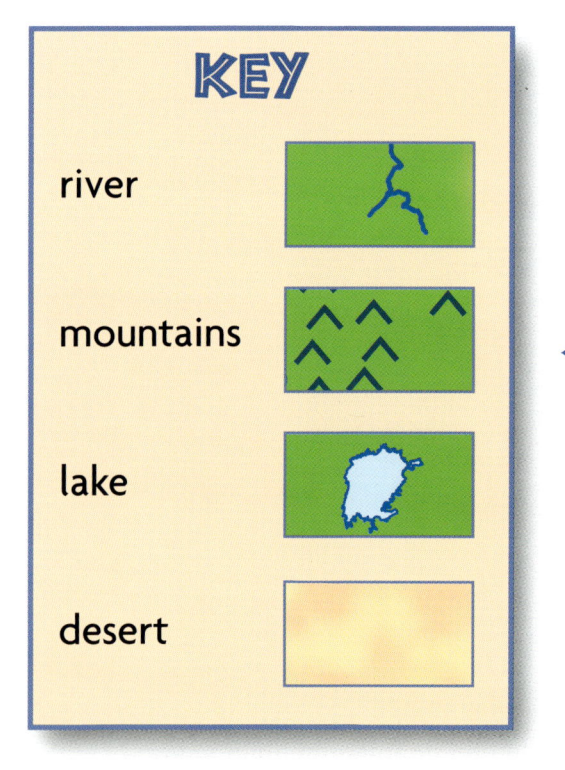

KEY

- river
- mountains
- lake
- desert

◀ These symbols can be on a map key.

KEY

river

mountains

lake

desert

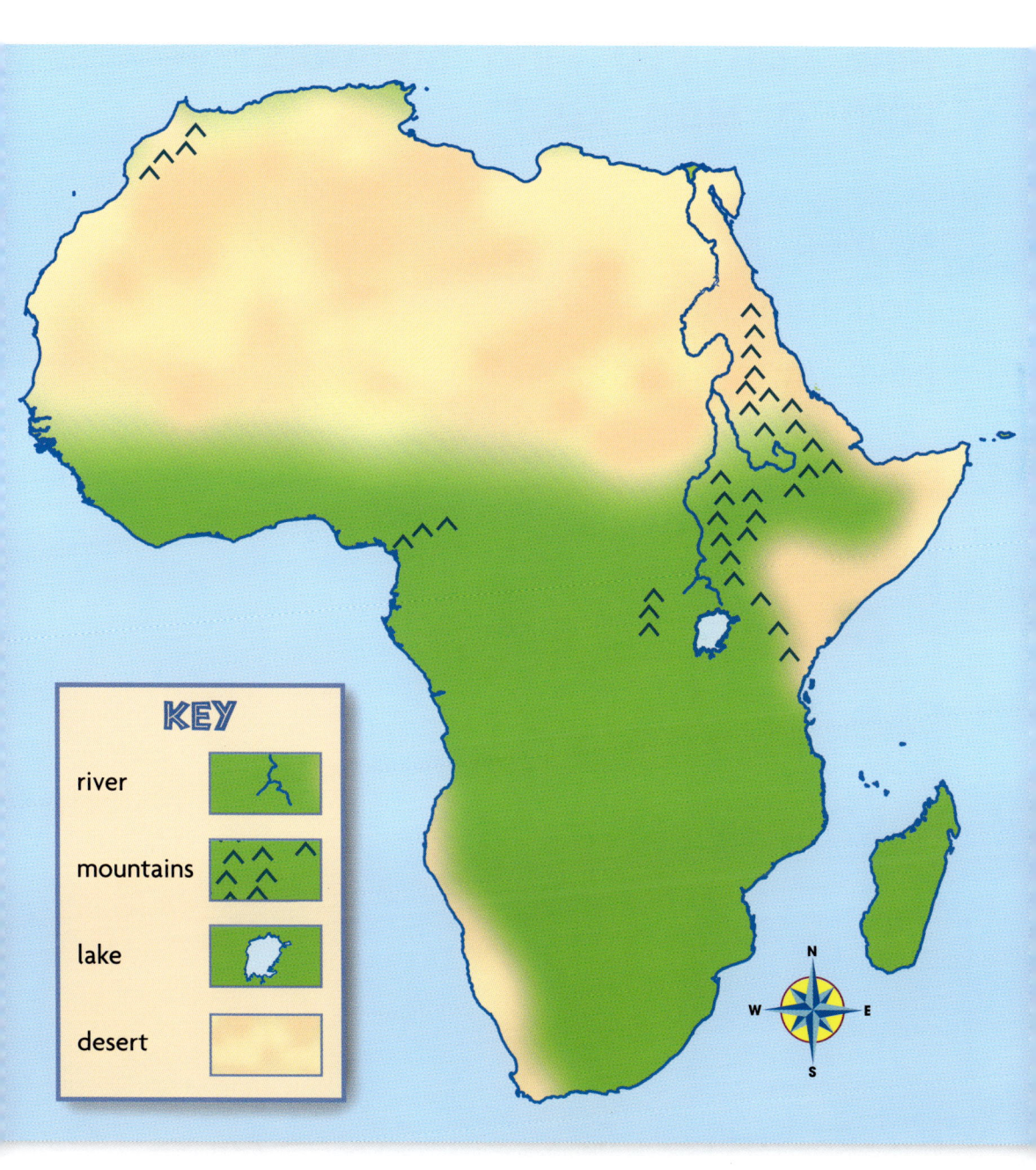

▲ What landforms can you find on this map? Look for the symbols.

How Can You Find Symbols with a Map Key?

A map key can help you locate the mountains in Africa. Africa does not have many mountains.

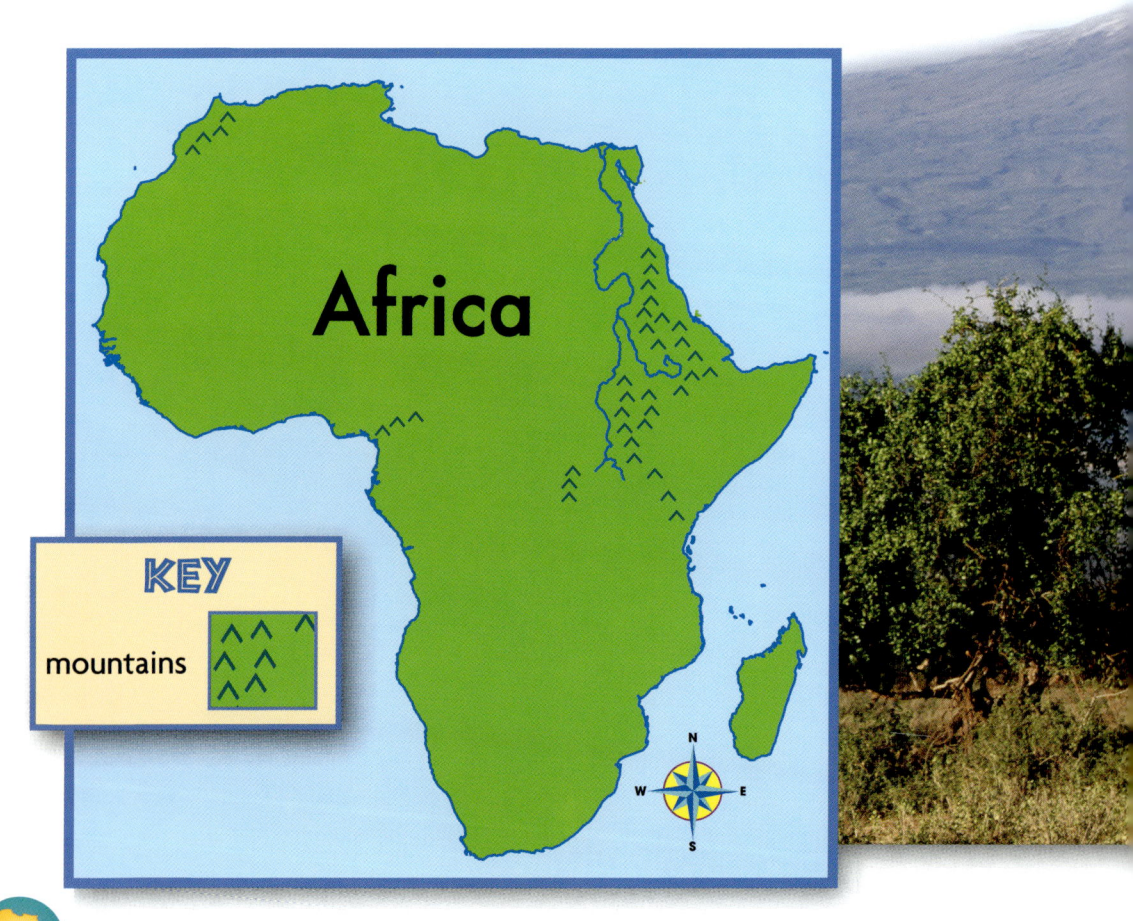

The tallest mountain in Africa is Mount Kilimanjaro.

▲ Grasslands grow around Mount Kilimanjaro.

Africa has a large **desert**. The desert is the Sahara Desert. It is dry and hot.

▲ Temperatures in the desert are very hot.

A map key can help you locate the Sahara Desert.

▲ The Sahara Desert is the largest desert in the world.

You can use a map to find many places. You can use a map key to locate **cities**.

▲ The city of Cairo is the capital of Egypt.

A map key has a symbol for roads, too. A map key helps you read maps.

KEY
road
city
capital

Alexandria

Egypt

Cairo

▲ A map can show the routes between cities.

Glossary

city (SIH-tee):
a place where people live that is bigger than a town
See page 14.

continent (KAHN-tuh-nehnt): one of the seven large pieces of land on Earth
See page 4.

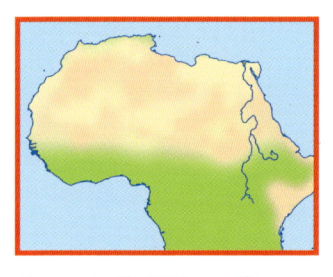

desert (DEH-zert):
a very dry area that receives little rain
See page 12.

landform (LAND-form):
a natural shape on the surface of Earth
See page 8.

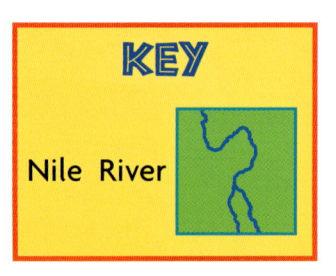

map key (MAP KEE):
the part of a map that lists the symbols on the map
See page 6.

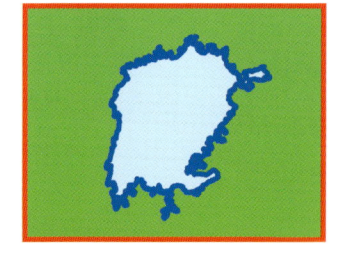

symbol (SIM-bul): an object or picture that stands for, or represents, something else
See page 6.

Index

Cairo, 14–15
cities, 14
continent, 4, 10
desert, 12–13

Egypt, 14–15
landforms, 8
map key, 6, 8, 10, 13–15

Mount Kilimanjaro, 11
Nile River, 5–6
Sahara Desert, 12–13
symbols, 6–8, 10

16